THE
NBA
A HISTORY OF HOOPS

Published by Creative Education
P.O. Box 227, Mankato, Minnesota 56002
Creative Education is an imprint of The Creative Company
www.thecreativecompany.us

Design and production by Christine Vanderbeek
Art direction by Rita Marshall

Printed by Corporate Graphics in the United States of America

Photographs by Dreamstime (Munktcu), Getty Images (Bill Baptist/
NBAE, Andrew D. Bernstein/NBAE, Walter Bibikow, Andy Hayt/NBAE,
Fernando Medina/NBAE, Layne Murdoch/NBAE, Joe Murphy/NBAE,
SM/AIUEO, Thinkstock, Jeff Vinnick/NBAE, Rocky Widner/NBAE),
iStockphoto (Brandon Laufenberg)

Library of Congress Cataloging-in-Publication Data
Pueschner, Gordon.
The story of the Memphis Grizzlies / by Gordon Pueschner.
p. cm. — (The NBA: a history of hoops)
Includes index.
Summary: The history of the Memphis Grizzlies professional basketball
team from its start in Vancouver, British Columbia, in 1995 to today,
spotlighting the franchise's greatest players and moments.
ISBN 978-1-58341-949-6
1. Memphis Grizzlies (Basketball team)—History—Juvenile literature.
I. Title. II. Series.
GV885.52.M46P48 2010   796.323'640971133—dc22   2009034782

CPSIA: 120109 PO1093

First Edition
2 4 6 8 9 7 5 3 1

Page 3: Forward Hakim Warrick
Pages 4–5: Point guard Mike Conley (number 11)

THE STORY OF THE

MEMPHIS
GRIZZLIES

GORDON PUESCHNER

CREATIVE ⊙ EDUCATION

CHAPTER ONE

FOUNDING THE FRANCHISE

Memphis, Tennessee, was founded in 1819 by military officer James Winchester, judge John Overton, and future United States president Andrew Jackson. These men, and the many settlers who soon followed their lead, were struck by the beauty of the location, which featured wooded bluffs overlooking the mighty Mississippi River. Hoping that the settlement would grow into a powerful city, the founders named it after the ancient Egyptian capital of Memphis, which was located along another great river, the Nile.

During its first 150 years, Memphis, Tennessee, earned renown for its export of cotton and also gained fame for its part in the development of blues music. In recent years, the city has drawn millions of tourists eager to see Graceland, the home of legendary singer Elvis Presley. In the summer of 2001, a new

Long known for its music, cotton, and lumber shipping, Memphis lacked a major professional sports franchise until the Grizzlies arrived.

attraction arrived in Memphis: a National Basketball Association (NBA) franchise called the Grizzlies. That franchise, however, was not a home-grown—or even a U.S.—product. It started out far from the land of cotton, more than 2,500 miles to the northwest, in Vancouver, British Columbia.

The Grizzlies were born as an NBA expansion franchise in 1995 and named after western Canada's ferocious wild bears. The new club was owned by local businessman Arthur Griffiths, who appointed Stu Jackson, a former NBA and college coach, as the Grizzlies' first president and general manager. Jackson, in turn, hired Atlanta Hawks assistant coach Brian Winters as the team's first head coach.

To assemble most of their initial roster, Jackson and Winters selected 13 players from the existing NBA teams via an expansion draft. Among the pickups were point guard Greg Anthony, veteran shooting guard Byron Scott, and speedy swingman Theodore "Blue" Edwards. The club then looked to add a big man it could build around—ideally, a bruising center who could score, rebound, and connect with Vancouver's fans. The Grizzlies got all of those qualities in their very first NBA Draft pick, center Bryant "Big Country" Reeves of Oklahoma State University.

COURTSIDE STORIES

THE BIRTH OF A BEAR

Grizz, the Memphis team mascot.

WHEN BUSINESSMAN ARTHUR GRIFFITHS STARTED THE PROCESS OF BRINGING A PROFESSIONAL BASKETBALL TEAM TO VANCOUVER, BRITISH COLUMBIA, IN 1995, HE IN-TENDED TO CALL THE NEW CLUB THE "MOUNTIES," AFTER THE ROYAL CANADIAN MOUNTED POLICE, WHO WEAR STRIKING RED UNIFORMS, WIDE-BRIMMED HATS, AND TALL, LEATHER BOOTS. But the real Mounties objected to the use of their name for the team. So Griffiths and Stu Jackson, the team's president and general manager, had to go back to the drawing board, where they came up with the name "Grizzlies." The name seemed apt because grizzly bears roam parts of the rugged landscape of British Columbia. The big animals also reflect-ed a powerful nature, which is always desired in sports, as well as the heritage of western Canada. When the Grizzlies moved from Vancouver to Memphis, Tennessee, in 2001, many people thought the name would have to go. Polls taken in Memphis, however, indi-cated that fans did not want the name changed. Only the color of the logo and the uniform was modified, from Naismith (neon) blue to Memphis Beale Street blue.

FEW TEAMS PLAY THEIR WAY INTO THE NBA RECORD BOOKS IN THEIR VERY FIRST SEASON. The Vancouver Grizzlies did it—although not in the manner they might have hoped—with a 23-game losing streak that set the mark for the most consecutive losses in a single season. In 1996, between February 16 and April 2, the Grizzlies lost every single game. "Basically," Grizzlies guard Greg Anthony summed up during the streak, "we're a bad basketball team." It wasn't until they took on the Minnesota Timberwolves at home on April 3 that the Grizzlies decided enough was enough. Vancouver trailed by 12 points after 3 quarters. But the Grizzlies made a spectacular comeback by going on a 16–0 run, then veteran forward Blue Edwards hit the game-winning shot from the top of the key with less than a second left on the clock. "I think we'd forgotten what it feels like to win," Edwards said amid the celebration that followed. The Grizzlies' dubious record was matched two years later by the 1997–98 Denver Nuggets.

COURTSIDE STORIES

FEELING BLUE

Blue Edwards lofts up a shot.

Reeves had a strong inside game and a willingness to learn that earned praise from coaches and scouts around the league. "I've always liked his game," said Bill Walton, a former All-Star center and television analyst. "He's learned the physical part of the game. All the raw material, all the potential, is there."

Although Reeves and his teammates shocked the NBA by winning their first two games of the 1995–96 season, reality soon set in. The Grizzlies lost their next 19 before finally defeating the Portland Trail Blazers in overtime in their 22nd game. Injuries late in the season led to another downward spiral. This time, the club lost an NBA-record 23 straight games en route to a 15–67 finish. Still, Vancouver fans appreciated the nightly effort of their undermanned Grizzlies, packing General Motors Place for nearly all of the team's home games.

After the season, Jackson set out to reward those fans' faith by obtaining some help for Reeves. Before the 1996 NBA Draft, the Grizzlies traded for forward Pete Chilcutt. Then, with the third overall pick in the Draft, Vancouver selected versatile, 19-year-old forward Shareef Abdur-Rahim, who had decided to turn pro after only one season at the University of California. After the Draft, the team made another trade to obtain forward George Lynch and sharpshooting guard Anthony Peeler.

Abdur-Rahim was an immediate sensation. Combining nimble spin moves with a soft shooting touch, he paced the 1996–97 Grizzlies in scoring with 18.7 points per game to earn a place on the NBA's All-Rookie team. Still, Vancouver continued to lose in bunches, again limping to the worst record in the NBA. "The losing has been tough," Abdur-Rahim said at the end of the 14–68 season. "The only thing I can control is my effort and my attitude going forward…. You do your best, keep on fighting and keep on battling."

INTRODUCING...

BRYANT REEVES

POSITION CENTER
HEIGHT 7 FEET
GRIZZLIES SEASONS
1995–2001

BRYANT "BIG COUNTRY" REEVES WAS A DOMINATING PRESENCE, A SEVEN-FOOT GIANT WHO COULD IMPOSE HIS PHYSICAL WILL ON THE COURT. Reeves came from the tiny town of Gans, Oklahoma (population 208), where there are no hotels and where, Reeves said proudly, "We still don't even have a stoplight." This country boy with the buzz cut was selected by the Grizzlies in 1995 as their first-ever NBA draft pick. He had a solid rookie season and then stepped up his game in 1996–97, averaging 16.2 points a night, which earned him a 6-year, $61.8-million contract. But this contract came back to haunt the Grizzlies as Reeves struggled with weight and injury problems. Prior to the 1998–99 season, he reported to training camp 40 pounds over his ideal playing weight, and in 2001, a nagging back injury forced Big Country to retire. "I am grateful to the entire Grizzlies organization for their support ... throughout my career," Reeves said. "Playing in the NBA allowed this small-town country boy ... to share the court with the greatest players in the game."

After their two dismal seasons, the Grizzlies hired a new head coach: former Orlando coach Brian Hill, who had assembled an impressive coaching resumè by leading the Magic to an average of 47 wins a year over 4 seasons. The Grizzlies then upgraded their roster by selecting point guard Antonio Daniels with the fourth overall pick in the 1997 NBA Draft. At 6-foot-4, and with an 82-inch wingspan, Daniels was taller and slower than the typical point guard. But he also played with unusual determination, and the Grizzlies were willing to take a chance on him. "I've been a sleeper my whole life," Daniels said. "I didn't get recruited by big colleges. I know what I'm up against in the NBA. Other point guards are built lower to the ground; they're all a lot faster. But I think I can jump over them."

With Daniels, Abdur-Rahim, and Reeves leading the charge, the Grizzlies felt prepared to take big steps in 1997–98. But despite the optimism, Vancouver still mustered only 19 wins. Although the Grizzlies were getting better—finishing sixth in the Western Conference's Midwest Division, one spot higher than the two years before—they still lost too many close contests.

New talent continued to arrive. In 1998, the Grizzlies selected point guard Mike Bibby from the University of Arizona with the second overall pick of the NBA Draft. Bibby, a great ball handler who cared more about giving his teammates scoring opportunities than padding his own statistics, quickly established himself as an elite player, averaging 13.2 points and 6.5 assists per game as a rookie. But the team lost Reeves for most of 1998–99 due to a back injury and remained stuck in a rut, going just 8–42 in a season that was shortened to 50 games because of a labor dispute between owners and players.

The Grizzlies kept searching for that special player who could turn their fortunes around, and in the 1999 NBA Draft, they nabbed guard Steve Francis, who was known for his quick slashing ability and

SHAREEF ABDUR-RAHIM

ON SEPTEMBER 22, 2008, SHAREEF ABDUR-RAHIM RETIRED FROM THE NBA AS ONE OF THE MOST UNDERRATED PLAYERS OF HIS TIME.

Abdur-Rahim's career started when he left the University of California after only one year, and the Grizzlies selected the youngster with the third overall pick of the 1996 NBA Draft. He made an immediate impact in Vancouver as a silky-smooth scorer who could hit shots from anywhere on the court, setting a franchise record with an 18.7-points-per-game average as a rookie. In the 2000 Summer Olympics, he gained wider exposure by helping the United States' men's team capture the gold medal. In a 2000 interview, Abdur-Rahim talked about the pressure of taking shots in high-stakes games. "I think in those situations, I have enough guts to step up and take the shot, and if I make a mistake, I can deal with it. I don't look at basketball as pressure. Pressure is a man with a family and five kids and no job." Abdur-Rahim played in the NBA for 12 seasons (wearing the uniforms of 4 different teams) and was an All-Star in 2001–02.

highflying dunks. But Francis then threw a wrench into Vancouver's plans by publicly announcing that he would not play for the lowly Grizzlies. So, the Grizzlies moved quickly, orchestrating a 3-team, 11-player deal with the Houston Rockets and Orlando Magic that brought four players—forward Othella Harrington and guards Michael Dickerson, Brent Price, and Austin Carr—and several future draft picks to Vancouver. "We've brought in a lot of new guys and, with that, an overall attitude change," said Abdur-Rahim. "We not only got more talented, we got fresher attitudes and, I think, a good group of guys." Still, Vancouver's play on the court remained largely the same, and the 1999–2000 Grizzlies finished just 22–60.

INTRODUCING...

MIKE BIBBY

POSITION GUARD
HEIGHT 6-FOOT-1
GRIZZLIES SEASONS 1998–2001

BASKETBALL RAN IN THE BLOOD IN MIKE BIBBY'S FAMILY. Bibby's father, Henry, had been an NBA point guard who later served as an assistant coach for the Philadelphia 76ers. Mike entered the pros in 1998, when the Grizzlies picked him second overall in the NBA Draft out of the University of Arizona. "With Bibby, you have a guy who is clearly the best player at that position in the draft, who knows how to run a team, and has excellent shooting ability," said Grizzlies president Stu Jackson. "Although he's young, he's probably going to be a real good point guard in the future." Bibby proved Jackson correct as he quickly established himself as an elite player with savvy playmaking abilities and a knack for hitting clutch shots. In his first year, the point guard made the NBA All-Rookie team and led the Grizzlies in both assists and steals. "He's consistent, he doesn't make mistakes, and he can run, too," said Los Angeles Lakers point guard Derek Fisher. In 2001, however, when retaining Bibby with a new contract became too expensive, the Grizzlies traded him to the Sacramento Kings.

CHAPTER TWO

REBUILDING: PHASE TWO

Three new figures arrived in Vancouver in 2000. The first was head coach Sidney Lowe, who preached defense and teamwork as the keys to success. Also arriving north of the Canadian border were backup center Isaac Austin and forward Stromile Swift—Austin via trade and Swift via the 2000 NBA Draft. New general manager Billy Knight (who had replaced Jackson midway through the 1999–2000 season) described the athletic, 6-foot-9 "Stro" as "a young colt ready to stand in the winner's circle."

Reeves suffered a back injury in the 2000–01 preseason, and the frequently hurt big man posted modest numbers throughout the year. The center's decline was a major setback, but his teammates did manage some highlights. In one mid-season game, Abdur-Rahim poured in an assortment of

With his wide wingspan and impressive leap, Stromile Swift played bigger than 6-foot-9, sometimes even manning the center position.

outside bombs and short-range jumpers to net a season-high 36 points in a loss to the Dallas Mavericks. Then, during the month of February, the Grizzlies assembled a franchise-record five-game winning streak. Still, the negatives again outweighed the positives as the team stumbled to a 23–59 finish. With every defeat, Vancouver fan support continued to dwindle.

After that sixth season, a major shakeup took place in Vancouver. In one chaotic day in June, Abdur-Rahim was traded to the Atlanta Hawks for the draft rights to Spanish forward/center Pau Gasol; the club drafted Duke University forward Shane Battier, the college Player of the Year; and Mike Bibby was sent to the Sacramento Kings in exchange for Jason Williams, one of the league's flashiest point guards. These additions revamped the Grizzlies' lineup, but the biggest change was still to come. Less than a week after the 2001 NBA Draft, the league's Board of Governors approved the sale of the struggling Grizzlies to a group of businessmen in Memphis who had plans to relocate the club. So, the team said goodbye to the Pacific Northwest and moved from Canada to Tennessee.

The Memphis Grizzlies opened the 2001–02 season in their temporary home, the Pyramid Arena, with an eight-game losing streak. Sadly, halfway through the season, Reeves, still battling chronic back pain, decided to retire after just six and a half NBA seasons. "Bryant has been a tremendous player and an exceptional team member, and we will certainly miss his contributions to our organization," Knight said. "We really appreciate his hard work and dedication to the team throughout the years."

Although the Grizzlies finished their inaugural Memphis season just 23–59, the play of Gasol—who averaged 17.6 points per game and won the NBA Rookie of the Year award by leading all first-year players in points, rebounds, and blocked shots—offered hope to the team's new fan base. Forward Lorenzen Wright, a former University of Memphis star, also

INTRODUCING...

PAU GASOL

POSITION FORWARD / CENTER
HEIGHT 7 FEET
GRIZZLIES SEASONS 2001–08

PAU GASOL WAS A FORCE TO BE RECKONED WITH.

Standing 7 feet tall and weighing 240 pounds, this Spanish native could move, pour in baskets from the post, rebound, and even knock down free throws with great accuracy. He was often compared to another multitalented NBA star, forward Kevin Garnett, for his ability to handle the ball and create plays off the dribble.

"I think he's very versatile, a high basketball IQ, can pass, can shoot, catch, finish ... he's extremely talented," said star Los Angeles Lakers guard Kobe Bryant. In 2001, Gasol arrived in Memphis as the third overall pick in the NBA Draft, becoming (at the time) the highest-drafted foreign player ever. "It's the best day of my life," Gasol said. "All of my life I want to be in the NBA." Gasol didn't waste any time making his mark as he won Rookie of the Year honors while ranking ninth in the NBA in blocked shots. He remained a lethal low-post scorer for the Grizzlies for the next five seasons until he was traded to the Lakers in 2008.

impressed the hometown crowd with several big performances, including a 33-point effort against the Mavericks early in the season.

Before the 2002–03 season, the Grizzlies brought in Jerry West, a longtime player, coach, and executive for the Los Angeles Lakers, as Memphis's new team president. West came out of retirement for the sole purpose of building a struggling team into a contender. "This opportunity gives me a challenge to do something unique," West said. "I have always wondered how it would be to build a winning franchise that has not experienced much success."

Success remained in short supply as the Grizzlies opened the next season with eight straight defeats, and Coach Lowe was fired. Under new coach Hubie Brown, a veteran of the NBA sidelines, the Grizzlies lost another 5 games for a 13-game skid that was the worst start to a season in club history. But in a home game against star guard Michael Jordan and the Washington Wizards, an unlikely hero emerged to end the drought. Second-year point guard Earl Watson came off the Memphis bench to score a career-high 17 points. In the fourth quarter, with the game tied and barely two minutes remaining, Watson nailed a three-pointer from the top of the key to give the Grizzlies the lead and spur them to an eventual 85–74 victory.

MOVING TO MEMPHIS

Memphis's Beale Street, famous for its music and nightlife.

IN 1995, THE TORONTO RAPTORS AND THE VANCOUVER GRIZZLIES BECAME THE FIRST BIG-TIME PROFESSIONAL BASKETBALL TEAMS TO PLAY IN CANADA SINCE THE TORONTO HUSKIES IN 1946. But basketball in Vancouver did not last long, and the Grizzlies never came close to a winning season in their six years there. Low morale among fans and decreasing support from the community left the team in debt, and by the year 2000, owner Michael Heisley had begun shopping for a new home for his team. In 2001, NBA owners unanimously approved the Grizzlies' relocation to Memphis, Tennessee. Memphis's acquisition of a pro sports franchise was a long time in coming; the city had been a finalist for a National Football League expansion team in 1974 and 1993 but lost out both times. "This is an exciting day for the people of Memphis," said J. R. Hyde, a part-owner of the team who had played a major role in bringing the club to Tennessee. "It's time to turn our focus to building a competitive basketball team that will be a positive force in the city."

From there, the Grizzlies fought their way to a final mark of 28–54, their best yet. Gasol poured in 19 points a game to set the scoring pace, Williams led the team in assists, and forward Mike Miller, a former Rookie of the Year award winner with the Magic, added offensive spark with his long-range gunning. Although the team's eighth season ended with an eighth losing record, the Grizzlies seemed to finally be moving up.

Jason Williams (below) and Mike Miller (opposite) starred together for three seasons, Williams with his passing and Miller with his shooting.

CHAPTER THREE

THE PLAYOFFS AT LAST

The Grizzlies finally let out a roar in 2003–04, thanks in part to the addition of forwards James Posey and Bo Outlaw and the continued improvement of Watson. By the end of February 2004, Memphis had 30 wins, already a franchise record. On March 29, in a road game against the Atlanta Hawks, Posey netted a career-high 38 points—including a buzzer-beating three-pointer that forced a second overtime and led to a 136–133 Grizzlies win—that helped Memphis clinch its first playoff appearance. The driving force throughout the club's 50–32 run to the postseason, however, was Gasol, who used his agile moves and sweet jump shot to emerge as one of the NBA's elite scorers. "It's a great turnaround for the franchise," Gasol said about making the playoffs. "We've surprised ourselves. I can't believe where we are."

A valuable player off the Grizzlies' bench, baby-faced point guard Earl Watson surprised many defenders with his quick burst to the basket.

In the first round of the playoffs, the Grizzlies took on the defend-
ing NBA champion San Antonio Spurs, losing the first two games in
San Antonio. In Game 3, the Grizzlies' first-ever home playoff game,
Memphis trailed 95–93 with only seconds left in the fourth quarter. Miller
launched a three-pointer that would have won the game, but the shot
went just long of the rim as the buzzer sounded. That was as close as
Memphis would get to a taste of playoff victory, as it dropped the next
game to lose the series.

The Grizzlies were eager to achieve bigger and better things the next
season, yet they struggled early, opening just 5–7. Then, unexpectedly,
71-year-old Hubie Brown resigned on Thanksgiving Day, stating that his
health could no longer handle the day-to-day strain of NBA coaching.
The Grizzlies soon replaced him with Mike Fratello, former coach of the
Hawks. Fratello's squad continued to struggle before a strong 12–3 push
propelled them to a 45–37 finish, good enough to claim the eighth spot
in the Western Conference playoffs. Unfortunately, the Grizzlies were
again swept in the first round, this time by the Phoenix Suns. "It's hard
right now," Gasol said after Memphis fell 123–115 in Game 4. "Maybe

THE COMEBACK KIDS

James Posey puts up a jumper.

THE MEMPHIS GRIZZLIES HAVE STRUGGLED MORE YEARS THAN NOT, OFTEN HOPING TO WIN MERELY 20 GAMES IN A SEASON. But during the 2003–04 season, the Grizzlies became known throughout the NBA as the "Comeback Kids" as they rolled to an impressive 50–32 record. Memphis rallied to win 14 games when trailing after the third quarter, the most by any NBA team that season. In a January 19 game against the Houston Rockets, the Grizzlies trailed by eight in the fourth quarter, but forward James Posey rallied Memphis to a 16–2 run that won the game. "We just kept fighting and making big plays down the stretch," Posey said. "When it's crunch time, you have to be able to go for the ball, which we did tonight." Posey played the role of hero again on March 29 in a game against the Atlanta Hawks, scoring 38 points and hitting a buzzer-beating 3-pointer to force a second overtime en route to a 136–133 Grizzlies victory. "We refused to lose," said Posey. Eighteen days later, the Comeback Kids made their first-ever playoff appearance.

ON NOVEMBER 3, 2004, THE GRIZZLIES STARTED A NEW SEASON IN A NEW HOME: THE FEDEXFORUM, A $250-MILLION, STATE-OF-THE-ART ARENA BUILT FOR THE TEAM ON FAMOUS BEALE STREET IN THE HEART OF MEMPHIS'S ENTERTAINMENT DISTRICT. The arena was built with fine dining options, a sports bar, and the latest stadium technology. Because Memphis is renowned for its contributions to the blues and rock 'n' roll, the theme of Memphis music decorates the interior. There are hallways dedicated to gospel, blues, rock, rap, hip-hop, and original artwork from regional artists representing the music of Memphis. "A forum is a public place, and this arena will be a showcase for professional sports and family entertainment that will serve the Memphis area for years to come," said FedEx official Michael Glenn. On that opening night of November 3, a capacity crowd of 18,119 hoped to see the Grizzlies crush the Washington Wizards, but the home team lost, 103–91. Memphis fans had to wait until November 10 to see a home victory, when forward Stromile Swift and his teammates topped the Los Angeles Lakers, 110–87.

after watching and seeing yourself [in a replay of the game] you can learn, but right now it is just painful."

The Grizzlies continued to stockpile talent in the off-season, selecting Hakim Warrick, a swift, 6-foot-9 forward from Syracuse University, in the 2005 NBA Draft. Two months later, on August 2, the Grizzlies took part in the biggest trade in NBA history, a swap involving 13 players from 5 teams. In this mega-blockbuster deal, Memphis sent Posey and Williams to the Miami Heat for veteran guard Eddie Jones. In another deal, forward Bonzi Wells was shipped to the Kings for scrappy point guard Bobby Jackson.

The moves seemed to pay off early in the 2005–06 season, as the Grizzlies claimed victory in 13 of their first 18 games. But playing in the same division (now the Southwest) as the Spurs and Mavericks, both perennial NBA powerhouses, the Grizzlies wound up in third place with 49 wins. The mark put the Grizzlies back in the playoffs, but, once again, the Memphis faithful watched their club get swept in a four-game series, this time by the Mavericks.

After dropping to 0–12 all time in postseason play, the Grizzlies continued to tinker with their roster, trading forward Shane Battier to the Houston Rockets for Stromile Swift (who returned to the team for a second stint) and 6-foot-9 rookie forward Rudy Gay, who had been picked eighth overall in the NBA Draft. "We acquired one of the very best prospects from this year's draft," Jerry West said of Gay. "Even though he is a very young player at 19, the talent of this young man is phenomenal, and we are hopeful people will enjoy watching this kind of athlete."

FOR MORE THAN HALF A CENTURY, HUBERT "HUBIE" BROWN COMMITTED HIMSELF FULLY TO BASKETBALL, STARTING WITH AN AMATEUR PLAYING CAREER WHILE IN THE U.S. ARMY IN THE 1950S. He then moved into the coaching ranks, eventually leading the Atlanta Hawks from 1976 to 1981 and the New York Knicks from 1982 to 1987. He retired from coaching in 1988 and worked as a television broadcaster until 2002, when the Grizzlies persuaded him to once again pick up the coaching whistle. As the NBA's oldest coach at 69 years of age, he turned the Grizzlies around with his patient, instructional coaching style. During the 2003–04 season, the Grizzlies went 50–32 and made the playoffs for the first time in franchise history. "What Hubie Brown has done for our league in the last two years has been great," said Indiana Pacers coach Rick Carlisle. "He brought an injection of life into that Memphis franchise and made them a playoff team." Late in 2004, however, health problems forced Brown to hang up his coaching whistle again. The following year, he was inducted into the Basketball Hall of Fame.

CHAPTER FOUR

A YOUTH MOVEMENT

The 2006–07 Grizzlies' playoff hopes were effectively squelched before the season even began, as Gasol broke his left foot while playing for Spain in the summertime International Basketball Federation World Championship. He would miss the first 22 games of the season, and the Grizzlies went 5–17 in his absence. At the end of December, coach Mike Fratello was fired. Replacing him was interim coach Tony Barone, the team's personnel director, who had never coached an NBA game. With such instability, the Grizzlies ended up with an NBA-worst 22–60 record. Still, there were some bright spots. Gay gave glimpses of his terrific potential by averaging 10.8 points per game, and Gasol—once he returned from his injury—set career highs with 20.8 points and 9.8 boards a night.

Rudy Gay's above-the-rim style of play earned him an invitation to the NBA's Slam Dunk Contest during the 2008 All-Star Game weekend.

n the off-season, the Grizzlies hired Marc Iavaroni, former assistant coach of the Phoenix Suns, as their ninth head coach. "Marc is going to make an immediate impact on this organization, team, and city, and we are honored that he will be making his NBA coaching debut in Memphis," said Grizzlies owner Michael Heisley. The team also acquired 6-foot-3 guard Juan Carlos Navarro, a 27-year-old rookie from Spain who was known as a capable marksman and tough defender.

Unfortunately, the new Grizzlies looked a lot like the old ones, as the team sputtered to a 5–10 start in 2007–08. Still mired in a losing funk by the beginning of February, Memphis traded its best player, Gasol, to the Lakers for four players—7-foot-1 centers Kwame Brown and Marc Gasol (Pau's younger brother) and guards Javaris Crittenton and Aaron McKie—and first-round draft picks in 2008 and 2010. "We're a 13-win team, so when you're in that situation, you've got to make moves," explained Chris Wallace, who had replaced Jerry West as general manager in 2007. The Grizzlies continued to spiral downward, ending up 22–60 again.

Memphis kept wheeling and dealing as it sought a winning combination. In the 2008 NBA Draft, the club swung a trade, sending Miller and forward Kevin Love, whom it had selected fifth overall, to the Minnesota

Timberwolves for 6-foot-4 guard O. J. Mayo, whom Minnesota had grabbed third overall. Mayo was an offensive dynamo who had strutted his stuff for one superb season at the University of Southern California, netting 20.7 points per game as a freshman. After also obtaining burly rookie forward Darrell Arthur, the Grizzlies went into the 2008–09 season with one of the NBA's youngest lineups—the average Memphis starter was a mere 21 years old.

As had become typical, the Grizzlies struggled early in the season. A month into the schedule, however, they started to turn things around. On December 14, Memphis defeated the Miami Heat behind Mayo's 28 points, notching its fourth victory in a row. "Guys are really buying into what Coach has been telling us," said Grizzlies point guard Mike Conley. "And after you see team basketball gets you wins, guys make it a point to work on it."

INTRODUCING...

MIKE MILLER

POSITION GUARD / FORWARD
HEIGHT 6-FOOT-8
GRIZZLIES SEASONS 2003–08

MIKE MILLER WAS ONE OF BASKETBALL'S MOST SKILLED LONG-BOMBERS, ABLE TO KNOCK DOWN SHOTS FROM OUTRAGEOUS DISTANCES. Standing a long-limbed 6-foot-8, Miller could shoot over most defenders. He also believed in continuous self-improvement. "I've never seen a player work harder in my life," said Grizzlies general manager Jerry West. In one phenomenal three-game stretch early in the 2006–07 season, Miller was at his absolute scoring peak. In back-to-back games, he hit seven three-pointers. Then, in the third game, he nailed nine "threes" in a win over the Golden State Warriors, making him the first NBA player to drill seven or more three-pointers in three consecutive games since Dallas Mavericks sharpshooter George McCloud did it in 1996. In 2005–06, Miller won the NBA's Sixth Man of the Year award for his tremendous play off the bench. "Mostly it's coming in to make an impact," said Miller about his sixth-man role, "and when you leave the game, you make sure you put your print on the game." Miller was sent to the Minnesota Timberwolves in 2008 as part of Memphis's trade to obtain high-scoring rookie guard O. J. Mayo.

As the season played out, the explosive Mayo captured conference Rookie of the Month honors in April and led all NBA first-year players with 19.1 points per game. Gasol proved himself a mean inside force, Gay emerged as Memphis's "go-to" scorer in clutch situations, and Warrick developed into an outstanding sixth man, adding hustle and soaring dunks as he came into games off the bench. Still, the Grizzlies' inexperience showed as they finished 24–58.

Memphis added several key players before the 2009–10 season, drafting shot-blocking center Hasheem Thabeet, trading for burly forward Zach Randolph, and signing point guard Allen Iverson, a 10-time All-Star. Although the Iverson experiment failed miserably (the veteran guard playing just three games before asking for his release), Randolph earned his paycheck, becoming the club's leading scorer and rebounder. The Grizzlies started their 15th season with a 1–8 whimper, but they were soon piling up victories, improving to 25–21 by the end of January before finishing the year 40–42. "Zach has been the catalyst behind our turnaround," said Chris Wallace. "Other teams have to double-team him, so there's more room out there for O. J. Mayo and Rudy Gay to operate."

COURTSIDE STORIES

YOUNG AND HUNGRY

O. J. Mayo drives past a defender.

AT THE START OF THE 2008–09 SEASON, THE MEMPHIS GRIZZLIES HAD THE ALMOST UNHEARD-OF TOTAL OF THREE ROOKIES IN THEIR STARTING LINEUP: GUARD O. J. MAYO (21 YEARS OLD), POWER FORWARD DARRELL ARTHUR (20), AND CENTER MARC GASOL (23). Third-year "veteran" forward Rudy Gay (22) and second-year point guard Mike Conley (21) filled out the starting five. And although the club took its share of the expected lumps, its young players showed promise. In December 2008, Memphis went on a 4-game winning streak, scoring more than 100 points in each victory. "It's another step for us," Grizzlies coach Marc Iavaroni said. "They've picked up the intensity, and it starts with defense.… It's a combination of technique and spirit." The two players leading the charge were Mayo and Gay. While Gay provided leadership on the court, Mayo proved to be a point-scoring wizard with his outside shooting and aggressive assaults on the rim. The two were among the youngest team-mate tandems in the league in which both players averaged more than 18 points a game.

The Memphis Grizzlies have suffered through more than their share of hard times since their inception, enduring lengthy losing skids, a long-distance relocation, and playoff appearances that—through early 2010—had yet to produce a single victory. But like the men who settled Memphis almost two centuries ago, today's Grizzlies have high hopes, and they expect to brandish their formidable claws soon.

Although separated in height by a full foot, Mike Conley (below) and Marc Gasol (opposite) both contributed to a formidable Memphis defense—Conley with his quickness and Gasol with his size.

INDEX